DIORAMA

DIORAMA

Sandra Marchetti

STEPHEN F. AUSTIN STATE UNIVERSITY PRESS

Copyright ©2025 Sandra Marchetti

All rights reserved. No part of this publication may be reproduced, stored in a retrieval system, or transmitted in any form, or by any means (electronic, mechanical, photocopying, recording or otherwise) without the prior written permission of the publisher.

Please address correspondence to Permissions:

Stephen F. Austin State University Press
sfapress@sfasu.edu

ISBN: 978-1-62288-283-0
Cover art: "A31: Tennessee Entrance Hall, 1835"
            by Narcissa Niblack Thorne, c. 1940.
Cover design: Brian Mihok
Managing Editor: Kimberly Verhines

for all of the artists I stole from, and for my husband

CONTENTS

∞

Shadow / *1*
Wakefulness / *2*
Refrain / *3*
Amberwing / *4*
Ion / *5*
Kaleidoscope / *6*
Northing / *7*
Semblance / *8*
Soon / *9*
Little Car / *10*
Seam / *11*
The Dream / *12*
Feather / *13*
Married Pairs / *14*
Westward / *15*

∞

Ebb Tide / *19*
Seven Sisters / *20*
Vision / *21*
Ice Chimes / *22*
Sunset / *23*
Glass / *24*
Imagination / *25*
Triptych / *26*
Satellite / *27*
Mother / *28*
Domesticity / *29*
Dream Only / *30*

Reservoir / *31*
The Book / *32*
Witness / *33*
"All that I can tell from here" / *34*
Tunneling / *35*
U.S. 41 / *36*

∽

Heirloom / *41*
Fall at Lake Ontario / *43*
Breath / *44*
Mise en Place / *45*
The Door / *46*
Equinox / *47*
Gibbous / *48*
Birthday / *49*
County Donuts / *50*
Depth of Field / *51*
Evensong / *52*
Of Late / *53*
A Swim at Europe Bay Beach
in July, Deserted / *54*

∽

Acknowledgments / *57*
Endnotes / *61*
Praise for Aisle 228 / *63*
About the Author / *67*

"At the end of my suffering
there was a door."

Louise Glück

Shadow

    "Something looks back from the trees," ~Jane Hirshfield

Mushrooms on the trail indicate
you haven't roved this prairie of late;

soft-sponged and pink, they're sweet
as the berries ripped in your teeth.

"Foxes are opportunistic feeders,"
notes a sign—I never mind

the goldfinches who arc my breeze
and swap big bluestem for trees

patiently trilling each leaf, those
last full masts of September.

Zig-zagged grass ripples from a felled
trunk, sunk in its thatch to rot.

Past piles of branches spoiled
to mash, a flaxen hay

wherein I catch your gleam—
spun gold you are a long-bodied

beam, slinking past imagined
houses down to the stream.

Hidden to your scruff in the gathering
dusk, I hold and release your stare,

that of a silver-eyed murderer
who smells breath in the air.

Wakefulness

I rise tonight to kiss your chest that tastes
of stain. Knowing I have nowhere to be

again, I cherish the days of our last mourning—
fires on the ground against dawn's sash.

I grant this past to you: sleep, the desk's
grain, a walk into the fogged tree line.

Against our sheets I shift, lie—content
to never be content as you, love, are.

Refrain

The birches dizzy me, shaking down
their mint and white confetti crowns around
the scarlet tanager, a trilling sky-high king:

red come orange, come black, come green.

From this forest freshed with song,
a goose lay drawn, opened
in a field ringed in feathers—

orange come red, come black, come green.

The coyote cast a wing
and three coronets
back to feign molting,

a confetti whorled white come red, come green.

Amberwing
Perithemis tenera

Hover over me,
fat-beaded miracle.

Swell your breast
clustered between

red-tinged wings
in autumn nearly

done opening.
Scan the grass

one last time,
dry as a stone,

as a woman alone,
climbing the stairs,

landing nowhere.

Ion

for Tracy K. Smith and Roger Reeves

It's a beautiful day
in America and we
are all waiting for
something terrible to happen.

A girl's balloon pops
on the commuter train
and we think it
is a gunshot.

The leaves we pass
sparkle with imaginary
dew. More people hold
books in their hands

than I have ever seen.
At the poetry reading
you discussed
lynchings in Paradise.

On this beautiful
suburban day,
all I can see is
lucid unease

once we've talked about
death, a feathered
final breath of the higher
self, unstable, seeing.

Kaleidoscope

We're warned all water drains
to rivers. Over sewers, fathers who escape
the house wash hands after weeding.

The runoff teems the flow:
Dillard's fish flashes then
dissolves like so much.

On the bank, men's shadows
beam as black bears
might upend themselves,

rocks in the stream,
their furred mouths
gleaming with the catch.

Northing

We effort
through cracked
crystals dusting
a ladder

green grew
through last
September. The snow
now higher

than the grass,
sentinels waiting
to relieve
each other.

Sound shuts
off like a stopped
bell, the ring
poured out.

In this room
where I am
alone it too
is winter.

Semblance

Easter's pale pink, green, lilac, blue:
I mute you. I will not sing across
hay-thatched grass as the songbirds do.

I see in the hue of a winter not yet
gone. The sun slips from stripped
trees and between the irises

Glück does not remember
the daffodils, gentle in their clusters,
clutching at the yellows of their throats.

A couple playing catch slides
from view; still the diorama
assembles, the scene runs true.

Soon

So shot with stalks
I can't see the garden
claimed from rock.

I will not press flesh
to grass, ruffled
thick to green, sleep

a finch feathered
through each fist.
My foot slips—

china, discarded
under moonbeam.
I limb the path, black;

across the rim,
the petals of a rose
close at the edge.

Little Car

Your car drove alone in the dark on the drag and all I could see was the flat black of it—some fool tossing matches out the window—your bumper bright liquid at night, breezing to the triangled horizon. Made of milk from stars and headlights, I am the lit wind scribbling your car, the match marring the ground—a burned underpinning—

Seam

Some night-
mare where
your lips
match mine—
humid, sick,
and swollen—
I am inside
our own dark
mouth, pumping
black sphere,
a pond where
goldfish breathe
a broken open O,
O. So big, a heart,
yours crack
as they part
with mine, caught
in the edges.

The Dream

It might
have been

a blue eye
snapping

shut; your
eyes snapped

shut and
opened again.

Feather

I come to
find it is
off the wing,
among the longest
on the bird,
a pattern only
found in males.
Barred white
and brown-
grey, I hold
it in my hand—
a scratch, a sail
as long as my
arm. How I
sat there as
you wept,
unable to move.

Married Pairs

    "…I mount the…
tunnel sunken night in search of you."
       ~Li-Young Lee

The last time, snow
fell from under the El
tracks like glitter,
like sugar, like fire,
or the rain.

                         I raised my
               hands parallel to the side-
               walk, to the tracks, and when
               the flakes came, I knew I could
                    do nothing to hold you.

Westward
for A. M.

Lip the rivulet, cold,
brown, and old;

your glow glints from
the collapsed town limits.

I ride on toward my
anonymity's wildness;

I roam the city
murmuring I am

young, my heart is strong,
and I can take it.

Ebb Tide

Spiders wind behind limestone
at heights twice mine.

A black beach brines
the vine-choked wall,

times my dizzied pull
at the horizon line.

~

I tell you this time I am not afraid.
I click the teeth of seven gods,

catch vines in my throat
and spit them to the sea.

I tell you I spark into fire
the grass behind my strides.

Seven Sisters

What are mountains
but lichen-backed
rocks, crevassed blue
flocks? I made

it back to you,
howling pack, flat
capped jacks, thrust
up bottle caps,

blades. Come, smooth
others, rough sisters;
like a jay cranes
his beak to the tree line,

I'm farther in than
I've ever been. In the fog,
a stand of pines—
mulched sculptures

divined on their sides.
This scream at your crags
divides to a track,
a seam I itch

to rumble through;
lead seven, you pull
the blue, mouth
the breeze, grab me.

Vision

I have
a fresh
heart for
you. My
lashes flick
in sleep,
slip my
limbs. My
spine unlocks
like a chime.

I press in
to our lie,
exhale my
mouthful
of fog.

Ice Chimes
    "Adazzle, dim" ~*G.M. Hopkins*

Like a blown glass chandelier's crash,
    slick bulbs sway, enflame the breeze—
        bowed limbs flare and start,
            singing their part in a roused dark.

Dipped river lanterns clank as knockers
    slaking off the snow—against
        the quarried lime, ice on the low-
            hanging branches scrims this flow.

Swell your chest to the carillon's mass
    beyond; as brass bells go on
        chiming, your story slips off
            and is gone.

Sunset

I turn to park my car somewhere
you would have found it, prop

my feet on the dash and listen
for the white throated songbird,

flexing its own chords. Like a cyclist
who dips beneath a branch at speed

or the softball field that's been seeded,
the diamond still a lighter green,

I've sunk back, not expecting to be seen.
In your traveling century,

it's impossible I'd still be
here, roaming like the ghost of me,

me at 13, then 23. I listen for you
in the lot, but can no longer see.

Glass

They reminded me of you.
The two housekeepers,
older women from the deep
South, scraping insects
from the windows
with a razor blade.

You held a college
degree, cleaned houses
through your pregnancy.
Lugging the vacuum
up each stair, mother—
you were fastidious.

They ate peanut butter
and jelly, went out to smoke
and flirt, but minded
their work—they checked
and double checked for you
in each window pane.

Imagination

I listen to your fishing
story and wonder,
does anyone cook
the catch anymore?

I saw you pat one's
side, glide it back
into the stream;

you were bound to be
Bishop's Riverman,
called to the current.

I imagine rainbows
or maybe a brook
trout you sought

but then thought
insignificant. How long
did it hang on
your hand, gleaming?

You flipped it
to the shallows
with a plop

I hear miles and
years on. I know
the fish has leapt

on its back, thinks
itself a river
dolphin again.

Triptych

I wait for a note
to float off the high
branch, to sing
and stay. All things
are migratory—
leaves on trees,
feathers molting.
The geese cannot
live in their coats
much longer.
The gray, brown,
and white glow
in my sight
lines, billowing
puffs of winter.
Their necks wander on
toward dusk, toward
time, the endless
crest of the preserve.

Satellite

It is night when I visit
here, not far off the lake
curling into my sneakers,
breakers and whitecaps
silent at this distance.
There is so much noise
out there. Stars wink
out over the horizon
and they are gone, gone—
maybe not stars at all.
On this anniversary
of nothing I see your face
vanish over the water
and it is love, not
your body, that is missing.

Mother

When you say
you are nearly home,
I look out at snow
on the blossoms,
strong sun ahead
of the cold. You
have forged me well,
assigned my worries,
taught me to care
for plans as they
dissolve like paper.

I carry your nerves,
those lengthy catalogues,
as sparks in my pocket,
flashes I scatter
to scar the ground.

Domesticity

Write about something true, like
the cough coming from beyond the room.

We drove all day on freeways
past strip malls and freight trucks

to get your medicine. It wasn't
sublime like the lizard scurrying

up the concrete stair, or the slug
paired with its trailing sheen.

Feeding chickens isn't glorious,
but rinsing your shoes in the hose is.

This farm is billed as topiary—
thatched Zen. My cohorts watch

the dumb animals eat
and I walk back in.

Dream Only

The lake a lilac cube. Lilacs suffuse the air bare in the noon heat. I smell their rum and sneeze in the sun, run from the pollen drowsing at their square pits, the split of a fist. Each one, four. No more petals on the face, one mirrored length.

Reservoir

Roots in the water
entangled my legs
as I swam up to
a stone for breath.

I talked to a couple
of guys baiting
lines slimed by
the depths, surrounded.

When I waded out
further, the green
nets swept around
and carried me—

I opened my eyes
underneath to see
aquas and blues glow
briefly to mystery.

Others said the vines
crept like eels
on the skin, tugs
toward total immersion.

I thought how novel
that someone sipped
from this, a tendril slipped
between each breath.

The Book

> "Glamour
> in retrospect
> involved false
> conception." ~*Brian Dettmer*

How much less did we expect
of knowledge before you?
In our hands,
the bland foretelling.
Left to right,
we read until
figures emerge.

Between the parentheses
I smell the whole,
open and decaying.
Like dried bread,
a greened coin,
or mold—I am
at the center.

A friend told me
about her favorite
library in India—
how the books
were eaten
through with
silverfish.

Witness

A fat snake
swiveled down
a branch
into the river
and I wondered,
what if I had
missed that?
I said to a
girl, "They're
usually not
that big,"
sure she had
seen it flop,
but she said
"Thank God
I did not.
I would have
screamed
bloody murder!"
I walked on
smiling, tracing
the thing's
path, its
inevitable
disappearance.

"All that I can tell from here"
~James Galvin

From here the rocks
cause bruise blue
skin; mosquitoes prick
me as I swim in.

A map notes you and I
span 3,000 miles,
pin to pin; farther
we have never been.

A valley unclasps
beyond my hands.
I anchor my skin
above the rocks and slide
in the cooled blue,
an ache away from you.

Tunneling

I leave my seat
and walk beneath
the stadium
expecting to find
daylight. Cool
as a cave,
sound fades
at this distance.

I bend to meet
the chanterelles,
clean as sponges
between my fingers.
I eat them tubed
within the blackness.

U.S. 41

On the second full
of the second season,
the rose-blue moon

stops Chicago
like a cork.
Bicycles chase

the lake. I ride
the starred Drive,
a carpet vacuumed

up to the Drake,
to lakeshore condos.
It's a scape

of bracken beaches
punched through
with legs.

Water begs
them, pedaling
to the lume.

They wait on
the lozenge
to flick and plume.

Come, otherworldly
and complete—
a wheel of flaked

stars, a dock
off a manicured
sandbar.

The city
erodes outside
my pillbox car.

Tonight the waves
thin in the moon,
cast my pink skin blue.

Heirloom

The sandpiper stares at the pickled sky,
whetted for tornadoes. Wind planes
off the plants, atrophied in their pots,

abreast to the thunderhead. I water,
and the leaves play harbinger rain
on my legs. Light washes the sandpiper,

knees high, white ruff to the wind.
A flicker on takeoff, then the screen
door springs open and I am in.

~

I finger the stems, the veins that pulse
blank chimes as a stream winds
from my watering can through the dirt.

Morning-gold leaves now skirt
the balcony, accordion from planters
to rail, like water striders.

~

And the limbs try on new souls,
scheme my hands to the soil that turns
my blood. I pick apart the stuck

buds, the spider's lace of roots
tubed from the black, the original
feed. I bleed, strum the seed,

my fingers spool as if returning
from sleep. A white feather,
the fuzz of fronds, a green bulb, then
a small fruit—red as my thumb.

Fall at Lake Ontario

Rivers lead to larger bodies,
a permeable sky overhead.

My hands know the turtle's
glide, forced up through

the shallows again. Each swimmer
a glaze-slicked shell

in the sun, setting
his own time.

Breath

Tonight the library is near
silent: just a soft-blown breeze
the ducts receive, a brittle wind
within the stacks.

I want to read Strand's "The Untelling,"
or of Hirsch's loss as he crossed
the Chicago River, drawing in
cotton candied air with his grandfather.

I want to hear the suck
of the air through the vents
and breathe, suffocated
by the sweet of it.

Mise en Place

Palm the whole
and slice in two.
Grip the knife
and circle the fruit.

Pink, white, or
yellow inside—
the flesh brims
up like sunrise.

Pare the segments
each into each
and wonder how
your parents

found the time
to work the blade
in 51 lines
for you to eat

the grapefruit
as you still do—
one triangle at a time,
cut to suit.

The Door
after LG

A frozen field,
the marbled lake.

What I don't know
is that you

have laid all
of this before me.

You stand behind,
eyes wide as a raptor's.

I create a carpet
of ice between us.

I want to say,
this is the end

of happiness. Will
I accept love?

Equinox

Shadows cross over
my head, then both of ours.
The bower dots the edge
of a spinning sky. How
much more tumbles on
before us: citrus pink, a fresh
breasted blue, and lavender
falls down like powder.

A drizzle begins,
then handfuls held
and dropped. Under
the eaves you slick
rain from me;
pollen bursts and flies.

Gibbous

A column of light
smeared in Degas
style. Japanese paper
hanger's moon
through clouds.
Like a plume
of lemon in water
or champagne
in a new flute,
lumen sinks to
ascend. A bee
slips the glass,
blinking within,
brights bubbling
from the hand.

Birthday
      after AS

The boatman
was a bus driver
who brought us
down from Anacapri

to the beach
when we said
we had no interest
in touring the Blue Grotto.

We changed
at a bodega
next to the corner
of sand and swam off.

It was cool, nearly
summer, and you
retired early
to watch.

I fixed my goggles
to see yellow
angels escape
me, a crown

swirling to account
for itself.
I touched water
the color of Windex.

Locked in the changing
room—laughing with
shame—we may have
buoyed the sky.

County Donuts
Schaumburg, Illinois

Sugar caked on my lips
slips through the air
like crystal ice, the way
glitter might. Fried dough
soft as a spell in my
mouth agape at the tray
sliding into the case.

The cook plops the dough
onto the conveyor belt
of steam, to bathe it in grease,
visible through his picture window.
Our bodies stop and breathe
after travelling a dozen
miles to play nighthawks in his scene.

Depth of Field

From above
filaments form
a branch
circling in
the pond.

At eye level
it's dirt
in standing
water, filtered
through light.

If survival is
hope by another
name, cram
the blossoms
upon my tongue.

Evensong

On the 4th of July
I glanced up
from my barbeque

grate and saw
neighbors waiting
out sunset just

as they pleased—
sparklers arced
over a pool splash,

pedestrians clapped,
bike tires screeched
while speakers

blared, smoke
trailed off fireworks
above the clink

of beers. And I
wished this
for the neighbors

I couldn't see—
a hand in
the darkness

to black the sky—
a flickering
reprieve.

Of Late

The bluest feathers lie in my husband's
eyes—bespeckled gold and green—
furrowing back young yet astigmatic.

His lashes flick as I preen
the gray at his temples.

What wisdom he has to grow
old now—for his aging to be seen—
like my grandfather who combed snow

at thirty, skipped dinners
to hum the microchip into being.

My husband opens each
lid—these, carrots now steamed—
aware of each meal and its meaning.

A Swim at Europe Bay Beach in July, Deserted

The lake glints green
at the edge of nightmare.

It's world's end in the deep
bay, gray and stumbling.

The lake itself a tumbler, a boat
you bobbed upwards out of.

I am convinced now that more
than anything what we want

is to live forever. No one can
see us, smashed as sea glass, open—

the ants eating our cherries
at the shoreline.

Acknowledgments

I give my gratitude to the editors and staffs of the following publications, in which these poems—sometimes in different versions—previously appeared:

Appalachian Heritage:	"Shadow"
	"Refrain"
Atticus Review:	"Mother"
Connotation Press:	"Reservoir"
	"'All that I can tell from here'"
The Cortland Review:	"Satellite"
Ecotone:	"Breath"
	"A Swim at Europe Bay Beach in July, Deserted"
FEED:	"Equinox"
The Festival Review:	"Birthday"
Gargoyle:	"The Dream"
	"Witness"
The Hollins Critic:	"Tunneling"
Italian Americana:	"Seam"

MARY Journal:	"Gibbous"
Mead Magazine:	"Soon"
the museum of americana:	"Mise en Place"
New Mexico Review:	"Northing"
Ovenbird Poetry:	"Vision"
phoebe:	"County Donuts"
Pilgrimage:	"Wakefulness" "Evensong"
Quiddity:	"Ice Chimes" "Sunset" "The Book" "Fall at Lake Ontario"
River Styx:	"Ion" "Domesticity"
Ruminate:	"Depth of Field"
So to Speak:	"Imagination"
South Dakota Review:	"Ebb Tide"
Split Lip Magazine:	"Kaleidoscope" "Little Car" "Westward"
Still: The Journal:	"Amberwing" "Of Late"

The Stockholm Review: "Feather"

Sugar House Review: "Seven Sisters"
               "U.S. 41"

UCity Review: "Glass"
               "The Door"

Vinyl Poetry and Prose: "Triptych"

Waccamaw: "Heirloom"

Whiskey Island: "Married Pairs"
               "Dream Only"

Word Riot: "Semblance"

In addition, select poems in this collection previously appeared in two chapbooks, *Heart Radicals* (ELJ Publications, 2016) and *Sight Lines* (Speaking of Marvels Press, 2016).

Endnotes

"Refrain" (3) borrows meter from the Anglican hymn "Holy, Holy, Holy" by Reginald Heber, composed in 1826.

"Kaleidoscope" (6) borrows a sentence from Annie Dillard's chapter, "Seeing," in *Pilgrim at Tinker Creek*: "A fish flashes, then dissolves in the water before my eyes like so much salt."

"Northing" (7) references Virginia Woolf's *A Room of One's Own*.

"Semblance" (8) references Louise Glück's *The Wild Iris*.

"Soon" (9) borrows a line from Sylvia Plath's poem, "Edge": "…petals / of a rose close…"

"Little Car" (10) borrows its title from Apollinaire's Calligramme, "La Petite Auto."

"Westward" (15) borrows a line from Li-Young Lee's poem, "Eating Alone": "…The ground is cold, / brown and old…"

"Ebb Tide" (19) borrows imagery from Anne Sexton's "Her Kind."

"Seven Sisters" (20) borrows a line from Li-Young Lee's poem, "The City in Which I Love You": "…come, smooth other, rough sister."

"Vision" (21) is an ekphrastic poem after Félix Vallotton's painting, "Le Mensonge," from 1898.

"Imagination" (25) references Elizabeth Bishop's poem, "The Riverman."

"Dream Only" (30) borrows its title and a line from John Ashbery's "They Dream Only of America": "The lake a lilac cube."

"Reservoir" (31) borrows a phrase from Elizabeth Bishop's "At the Fishhouses": "...total immersion."

The title of "U.S. 41" (36) references the specific section of this route in Chicago known as DuSable Lake Shore Drive.

"Fall at Lake Ontario" (43) borrows a line from Sharon Olds' poem, "Sex Without Love": "single body alone in the universe / against its own best time."

"Breath" (44) borrows images from Edward Hirsch's poem, "Cotton Candy" and Mark Strand's poem, "The Untelling."

"The Door" (46) borrows its title from Louise Glück's poem, "The Wild Iris": "At the end of my suffering / there was a door."

"Gibbous" (48) references the influence Japanese prints made on Edgar Degas' style.

"Birthday" (49) borrows imagery from Anne Sexton's poem, "The Nude Swim."

"County Donuts" (50) references Edward Hopper's painting, "Nighthawks" from 1942.

"Of Late" (53) borrows a phrase from Carl Phillips' poem, "Clear, Cloudless": "the bluest feather."

"A Swim at Europe Bay Beach in July, Deserted" (54) also borrows imagery from Anne Sexton's poem, "The Nude Swim." Europe Bay Beach is located in Door County, Wisconsin.

Praise for Aisle 228
by Sandra Marchetti

Winner of the 2023 *Twin Bill* Book Prize
for Best Baseball Poetry Book of the Year

"'How can you not be romantic about baseball?' Sandra Marchetti's epigraph from the movie *Moneyball* asks at the start of this nostalgic collection. The 'national pastime' is certainly a sport of myth and legend. All sports are, but especially baseball. Among the oldest stories is the one about the Chicago Cubs, the perennial losers, the heartbreakers. The Cubs are Marchetti's team – the team of three generations of her family of Chicagoans. Divided into two sections, 'Losers' and 'Winners,' *Aisle 228* is a collection with a happy ending.

…You see the mallard that flies in and squats in short center field, the deference the players show the bird (in 'Invasive'). She extols the memorable personalities of the game, Bob Uecker, the voice of the Milwaukee Brewers, still going strong at 91, Harry Caray singing the seventh inning stretch song at Wrigley, Pete Rose, Ichiro Suzuki, Greg Maddux."

~Reviewed by Charles Rammelkamp
for *North of Oxford*

"*Aisle 228* begins in a familiar place for long-time Cub fans: in the days when the Cubs were still mired in the Curse of the Billy Goat. In the first poem, 'Frame,' Marchetti writes:

My father gripes and wipes his nose
through the April game—
the team terrible again—

yet players lope over this green hill
and our minds agree to rise
and clap for them.

Those words capture something fundamental about being a sports fan, especially a fan of a perennial loser — we return each year knowing we're gearing up for more heartbreak, but we still let some hope come out, we still clap for the players. It's a thought echoed in the final couplet of the book's second poem, 'The Unsayable' — 'We flicker in our seats, dimly/recede, but never leave.'"

~Reviewed by Justin Carter
for *Fansided*

"'I believe in the Church of Baseball. I've tried all the major religions and most of the minor ones…and the only church that truly feeds the soul is the Church of Baseball,' declares connoisseur of the game Annie Savoy in the movie *Bull Durham*. Sandra Marchetti agrees with her thesis, and shares her spiritual love of the sport in her new book, *Aisle 228*. In fact, Marchetti refers to this aisle in which she spent a good deal of her childhood with her father at Wrigley Field as 'a front row to Eden.' In the stands along the field, 'we pray… / The organ keys strike three, / abide the trinity.' A godlike figure's voice booms with the play-by-play as parishioners in the stands practice their customs and grapple with their superstitions. The game has nine innings, a pregnancy incubating from conception to birth, a wish to deliver a win and set the field alive."

~Reviewed by Elizabeth Strauss Friedman
for *Newcity Lit*

"Baseball is the cure for loneliness. Poetry is the cause. Writing can be isolating, pulling poets away from our communities and loved ones to toil at our desks. What a welcome diversion the ballpark can be, especially when the home team is doing well. 'Winners,' the second half of *Aisle 228*, follows the 2016 Chicago Cubs, who opened a portal to hell by winning the World Series that year. As Obvious

Shirts, a new t-shirt company founded by a Cubs fan to proudly state obvious opinions, phrases it: 'The greatest game ever played was on a Wednesday in Cleveland.' How odd! Communal celebration, alongside a sense of the supernatural, inhabits this section of the book.

Marchetti skillfully renders the emotional rollercoaster of being a fan. The important moments of a game happen quickly. In a double play, 'hands work the blur.' In a poem about defensive plays, a little magic has to be invited in. There is magic, but crying as well. Myths are busted. As the final play of the World Series concludes, she notes 'silence—then / a bursting beat.' The em dash and the gerund seem to invoke Emily Dickinson, whose 'After great pain, a formal feeling comes—' is resonant with the moment of epiphany. The poem ends, 'First – Chill – then Stupor – then the letting go.' Even though the Dickinson poem illustrates death, it suits the victorious situation well too. Certainly, Cubs fans felt a great pain in the 108-year drought between championships. And stupor definitely followed."

~Reviewed by Krystal Languell
for *Sugar House Review*

"When I think of baseball, I think of all the sounds: the 'thwack' of the baseball against wood, the organ music, the announcers, all that cursing! Marchetti, a master poet, weaves sound throughout this book, not only by poetic form and meter, but by her emphasis on sounds and their conveyance….Poetry as a part of baseball—or baseball's poetics—serves as a means to convey loss as well. The sport becomes numinous and ghostly….There is an elegiac quality to many of these poems, as if the speaker is attempting to reach back to older connection, much like tuning a radio dial. Baseball is a connection to the speaker's father and to her lineage…."

~Reviewed by Jennifer Martelli
for *Italian Americana*

"Sometimes a poem is about trying to get a radio signal; sometimes, about the loyalty of sticking it out for extra innings. Details of games, but also of post-game moments, like exiting the stadium in 'Denouement'—'A dozen doors thwack open / dull as scrapped cups.' The poem 'Relish' is a pun and a tribute to baseball food, the hot dog, the onions, the mustard (never ketchup!)."

~Reviewed by Kathleen Kirk
for *Escape Into Life*

About the Author

SANDRA MARCHETTI is the 2023 Winner of *The Twin Bill* Book Prize for Best Baseball Poetry Book of the Year. She is the author of two full-length collections of poetry, *Aisle 228* from Stephen F. Austin State University Press (2023) and *Confluence* from Sundress Publications (2015). Sandy is also the author of four chapbooks of poetry and lyric essays, including *Sight Lines* (Speaking of Marvels Press, 2016), *Heart Radicals* (ELJ Publications, 2016), *A Detail in the Landscape* (Eating Dog Press, 2014), and *The Canopy* (MWC Press, 2012). Sandra's poetry appears widely in *Blackbird, Ecotone, Subtropics, Southwest Review, Poet Lore*, and elsewhere. Her essays can be found at *The Rumpus, Pleiades, Mid-American Review, Barrelhouse, Whiskey Island*, and other venues. Sandy is the Poetry Editor Emerita at *River Styx* Magazine. She earned an MFA in Creative Writing—Poetry from George Mason University and now serves as the Assistant Director of Academic Support at Harper College in the Chicagoland area.

www.ingramcontent.com/pod-product-compliance
Lightning Source LLC
Jackson TN
JSHW021958080425
82250JS00003B/18